THE MAN WHO COULDN'T SEE

Ella K. Lindvall

© 1982, 1994 by
THE MOODY BIBLE INSTITUTE
OF CHICAGO

This story has been extracted from
Read-Aloud Bible Stories, vol. 1

Illustrated by
H. Kent Puckett

Printed in Mexico

MOODY PRESS

Poor Bartimaeus.
His eyes were sick.

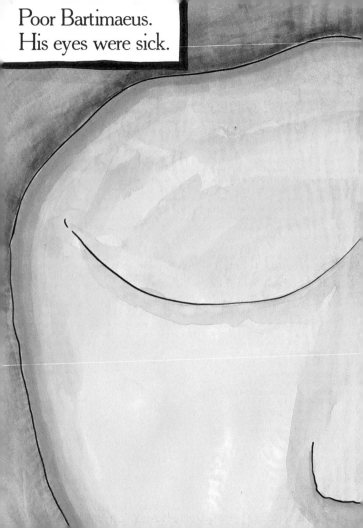

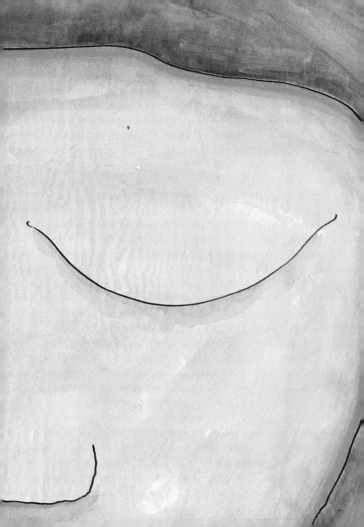

He couldn't see the sun.

He couldn't see the trees.

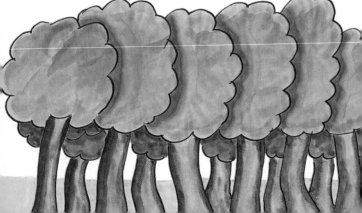

He couldn't see the houses.

He couldn't see people.
But Bartimaeus could hear.
And one day —

He heard lots of people walking.
Step. Step. Step.
He heard lots of people talking.
Talk. Talk. Talk.

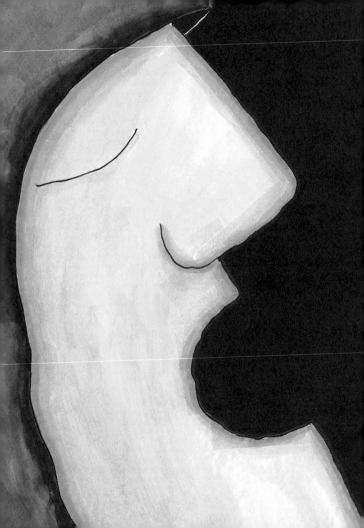

"What is happening?"
asked Bartimaeus.
"What is happening?"

"It's Jesus," somebody said.
"Jesus is coming down the road.
We're all walking with Him."

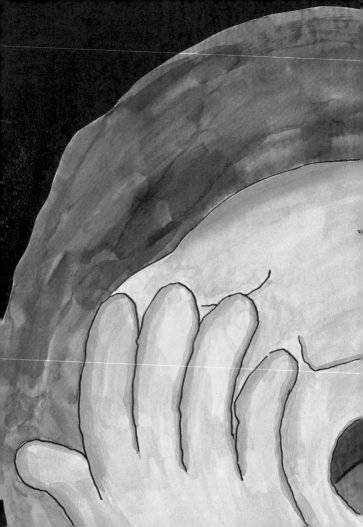

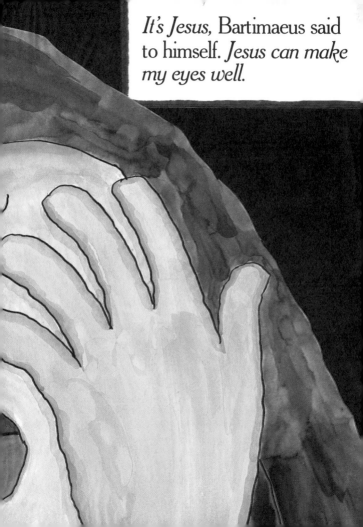

It's Jesus, Bartimaeus said to himself. *Jesus can make my eyes well.*

"Jesus!" he called. "Help me!
Jesus, help me!"

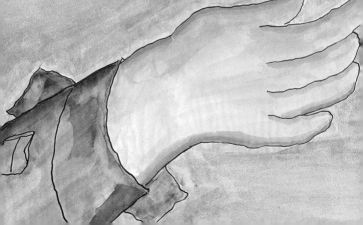

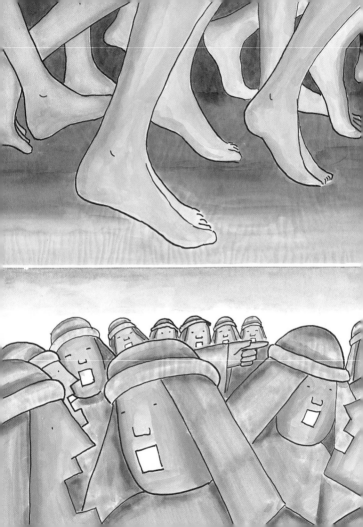

Now, lots of people were making noise walking.

Lots of people were making noise talking.
BUT—

JESUS HEARD BARTIMAEUS ANYWAY,
and Jesus stood still.
"What do you want me to do
for you?" He asked kindly.

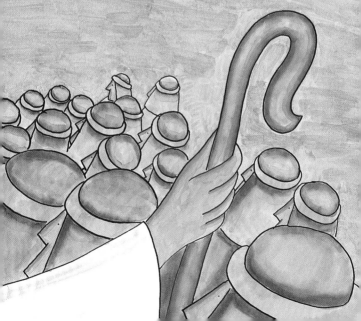

I'll tell you what Jesus said.
He said yes.
"You may see," He told Bartimaeus.
And all at once —

Bartimaeus saw the sun.
Bartimaeus saw the trees.

Bartimaeus saw the houses.
Bartimaeus saw the people.
But best of all—

Bartimaeus saw Jesus.

What did you learn?

Jesus hears when people
talk to Him.
He heard Bartimaeus.
When you talk to Jesus,
He hears you, too.

About the Author

Ella K. Lindvall (A.B., Taylor University; Wheaton College; Northern Illinois University) is a mother and former elementary school teacher. She is the author of *The Bible Illustrated for Little Children*, and *Read-Aloud Bible Stories*, volumes I, II, III, and IV.